Sue Porter's Guide to

RUGBY

A handbook for bemused supporters

Ann Waterhouse

Illustrations by Amanda Stiby Harris

ISBN 978-0-9574573-0-0

This edition published in 2012 by
Ann M Waterhouse Ltd
email: info@sueportersguide.com
www.sueportersguide.com

A previous edition of this book was published in 1995 by Souvenir Press
Ltd., with variations in the text and illustrations, as part of a book entitled
Rugby & Cricket for Mums.

The first edition of this book, with variations in the text and different
illustrations, was first published privately in 1994 by Caterham School,
Surrey, under the title Rugby for Mums.

A CIP catalogue record of this book can be obtained from the British Library.

Printed in the UK by Imprint Digital

Dedication

This book is dedicated to that hardy band of supporters - or should that be Sue Porters - but mostly parents and grandparents, who brave all the appalling weather the British Isles can throw at them, to watch a bunch of grubby small boys or girls doing their best to kill each other each week (or so it seems to the uninitiated).

Contents

Acknowledgements

The author would like to thank:

Caterham School, whose myriad sporting activities inspired her to write the first edition of this book as a guide for its bewildered mothers.

The late Stephen Smith, former Headmaster of Caterham School and an England scrum-half, without whose early support this book would probably never have been published.

All the Caterham School sports masters, especially Pat Lavery and John Moulton, for their help and guidance in the preparation of the original books.

Her husband David, without whom her interest in the game would never have been kindled in the first place.

Gareth and Alan for giving her a reason to stand on freezing cold touch lines for over ten years through every kind of wind and weather and still enjoy every second of it.

Amanda and her brother Robert for their invaluable help in the final edit and preparation of the book for publication.

And finally . . . the Elsted Inn in West Sussex, whose warm hospitality allowed Amanda and her to recreate this book in its current format.

Introduction

Why write a series of books on sport for parents and others who never played the games themselves? I must have been asked that question so many times since the appearance of my first booklet on the game of rugby. That was designed to inform and entertain the parents of Caterham School in Surrey, where my own two boys were enjoying multiple sporting activities in the guise of education.

There are of course many detailed books on the rules and techniques for playing this sport, but few of them are aimed specifically at the spectator, and none that we could find were aimed at parents or other relatives.

Any mother who has stood in the freezing cold on a rugby touch line will confirm that the more you learn about the game, the more enjoyable watching a match becomes.

So it was for me, and as my elder son's team was supported by parents with boys higher up the school, whose knowledge was greater than mine, I was only too grateful for small crumbs of wisdom that they passed on to me during the course of school matches.

As the years progressed, I gradually felt I was beginning to understand this exciting sport and in my turn I passed on some of my knowledge to the spectators watching my smaller son's matches. It was these good souls who kept saying, 'Why don't you write a book about it?' So it was all these experiences that inspired me to complete the books.

In general, I will explain the game in terms of a parent's view, but the advice in this book applies equally to boyfriends and girlfriends, wives and husbands. Since the book was originally conceived with boys' parents in mind, I will generally use he, his and him but please don't think this precludes the same information from applying to your young daughter if she's taken up the game at her local junior rugby club or school.

What is Rugby?

Origins and History

The game of Rugby Football, so history tells us, started in 1823 when a certain William Webb Ellis (a pupil at Rugby School) picked up a football and ran with it. After crossing the goal line he reportedly turned to his sports master and asked 'Is that a goal sir?' to which the master responded, 'No, but it's a jolly good try'.

This apocryphal tale has never been confirmed as fact, although this exchange is frequently quoted as the reason for a *try* being so named. However, the first official rules of the game were written down at Rugby School in 1845.

After these rules were published the game spread throughout England, and on 4 December 1870 Edwin Ash of Richmond and Benjamin Burns of Blackheath published a letter in The Times suggesting that 'those who play the Rugby-type game should meet to form a code of practice as various clubs play to rules which differ from others, which makes the game difficult to play.' On 26 January 1871 a meeting attended by representatives from 21 clubs was held in London at the Pall Mall Restaurant on Regent Street.

The 21 clubs present at the meeting were: Blackheath (represented by Burns and Frederick Stokes, the latter became the first captain of England), Richmond, Ravenscourt Park, West Kent, Marlborough Nomads, Wimbledon Hornets, Gipsies, Civil Service, The Law Club, Wellington College, Guy's Hospital, Flamingoes, Clapham Rovers, Harlequin F.C., King's College Hospital, St Paul's, Queen's House, Lausanne, Addison, Mohicans, and Belsize Park. The one notable omission was the Wasps. According to one version, a Wasps' representative was sent to attend the meeting, but owing to a misunderstanding, was sent to the wrong venue at the wrong time on the wrong day. Another version is that he went to a venue of the same name where, after consuming a number of drinks, he realised his mistake but was too drunk to make his way to the correct venue.

The game continued to develop until 1895, when a major dispute over payments to players led to the formation of a rival organization, the Northern Rugby Football Union. These two organizations competed for control of the game, but neither succeeded. As a result, two forms of the game, or 'codes', developed. One was run by the Rugby Football Union and called 'Rugby Union'; players of this code couldn't earn money from the game (although nowadays they can). The other was run by the Northern Rugby Football Union and was called 'Rugby League', and players of this code were paid to play.

The two codes have slightly different rules, with the most important differences being the way play is continued after a player has been tackled and the number of players on each team: 15 for Rugby Union and 13 for Rugby League.

Rugby Union at the top flight finally turned professional in 1995, just after the first edition of this book was published, when the International Rugby Board (IRB) allowed payments to Union players for the first time in the game's history.

Players are now able to switch between the two codes without penalty over the course of their careers and rugby is now played by men and women, boys and girls, in more than a hundred countries across five continents. The IRB membership in 2012 totalled 97 Unions in full membership, 20 Associate Members and 6 Regional Associations.

Whilst the game of rugby originally developed from football, there are major differences between these two sports, apart from the most obvious one of being allowed to handle the ball. These include the H-shaped goalposts and the oval-shaped ball. A rugby game is made up of two halves that last 40 minutes each, with a short interval at half-time. At junior level this is rarely more than 5 minutes, but at international level it is usually 15 minutes.

The World Cup

The Rugby World Cup

Many new supporters come to the game of rugby after watching televised international matches, such as the Six Nations annual competition or the World Cup. The latter competition was instigated in 1987 to bring together the leading rugby nations in a four-yearly tournament, timed to occur the year before the Olympic Games. Nowadays rugby playing nations from around the world compete in the early stages.

The first round is a pool stage. The following format was used in 2003, 2007 and 2011: twenty teams divided into four pools of five teams, with each pool playing a round-robin series of ten games against the other teams in the same pool. Teams are awarded four points for a win, two points for a draw and none for a defeat. A team scoring four or more tries in one match will score a bonus point, as will a team that loses by seven points or fewer.

The teams finishing in the top two of each pool advance to the quarter finals. Then a further knock-out competition establishes who will get through to the final match. There are specialised websites telling you all about the Six Nations and the World Cup, if you'd like to learn more.

Scoring Points

The main aim of rugby is to score points (not goals, as in football). This is done by the team carrying, passing and kicking the ball to the opposition's goal line and touching the ball down behind that line to score a try, worth 5 points.

This is then *converted* if a player can kick the ball over the crossbar, between the goalposts, having previously placed it back on the pitch in line with the point where the try was scored. If the kick is successful, two more points are added to the score.

Alternatively, the ball can be kicked over the posts from either a *penalty kick* or a *drop kick* (kicking the ball after dropping it from your hands) in order to score three points. These are also described as penalty goals or drop goals.

For the past few years the points scored from the various plays have remained the same, but over the years the laws regarding scores have been changed on several occasions, so it's worth being aware of this.

Passing the ball away from the passage of play

Unlike most other sports, in rugby the ball must always be passed sideways or backwards (i.e. away from the passage of play and the opposition's *try line*). If the ball is passed forwards to a team colleague, this is called a *forward pass* and is penalised by the award of a *scrum*.

If the ball is dropped forwards (this is described as a *knock-on*) and if this action is considered to be unintentional, the referee will award a scrum to the opposition where the forward pass/knock on occurred. However, if the referee believes the knock-on or throw forward was intentional, a penalty kick is awarded instead, which could allow the opposition to score points immediately.

You can check out www.irblaws.com for full details of the laws of Rugby Union and detailed explanations of all the penalties that can apply in a game. This will give you a much more comprehensive idea if you are interested in learning more.

There is obviously lots more to learn about the basics of the game, but on the following pages we attempt to explain the positions on the pitch and their roles within a game. Words in italics in this book refer to items listed in our glossary at the back of the book, so if you want a quick explanation of a particular term, just flick to the back pages and you'll find it there.

The game is proud of its five core values - Teamwork, Respect, Enjoyment, Discipline and Sportsmanship. Every player - and indeed every supporter - should bear these five elements in mind when a game is taking place - they are key factors in every rugby game, wherever it is being played, and make the game what it is today, a vibrant, exciting and fun game to watch and play.

Playing Positions

Rugby Union teams consist of 15 players as opposed to a soccer football team of 11. School teams are often referred to as the First Fifteen, Second Fifteen, etc. (and this is sometimes written down in Latin as XV). Each team is split almost equally between players known as *backs* and *forwards*.

The forwards are mainly responsible for getting the ball down the pitch towards the try line using brute strength and techniques known as rucking, mauling and scrummaging, all of which we will explain in more detail later.

One of the most common forms of organised play for forwards, something you will see frequently during a match, is a type of group hug that seems like a team bonding exercise but is actually called a scrum (or *scrummage*).

The backs traditionally run with the ball in hand, passing it between themselves, and running down the pitch until they are tackled by the opposition. If they are tackled and trip or fall over and the ball touches the ground, they must either pass the ball (ideally to a fellow team member) or immediately release it for other players to pick up.

In recent years the differences in style of play between backs and forwards have been broken down and now senior players have begun to adopt each other's playing techniques. It's not uncommon for forwards to join the back line in attacking the opposition and backs nowadays frequently get caught up in the mauls and rucks that were previously the preserve of the forwards.

Your Child's Position

Almost the first question any parent asks their child when they start playing a new sport is 'So, what position are you playing?' This demonstration of supposed knowledge usually leads to you falling flat on your face when your child replies, 'I don't know, I think I'm a back' or 'I think I'm a forward'.

Since the game is new to them too it may take many weeks before they play in a consistent position on the field and develop any understanding of that role in the team; until then they will probably have no idea what position they are playing. Eventually however they will find their place.

For younger players, it is traditional for the large children to become forwards and the smaller or faster ones to join the backs. Later on this may all change as players change shape through teenage, and your slim little back can turn into a hulking brute of a forward over the space of a couple of rugby seasons.

However, it will generally remain true that if they move fast over the ground, they will become a back and if they tower over their peers or weigh a little more than average they could be more suited to the forwards group.

The smallest player on the pitch is frequently the scrum-half. Quite why the smallest player should be the one who has to get closest to the big heavy forwards we have never understood, but there it is.

Certain positions on the rugby pitch require particular physiques, and the following general descriptions may help you pick out a player at a glance as you start to watch your first season of rugby.

The Forwards

The players known as the forwards make up the three rows of a scrum: front row forwards, second row forwards and back row forwards:.

The Front Row Forwards

These include the hooker and the prop forwards (tight-head and loose-head). Tradition has it that forwards do not need the looks of a Hollywood film star to play well. To be an effective front row forward a player should preferably have very long arms and no neck. Players with normal arms and necks tend to play elsewhere – regardless of their looks.

Front row forwards are renowned for their volatile natures - they are best left well alone as they can become awkward if roused.

The Second Row Forwards (Locks)

The second row forwards help 'lock' the scrum together, but their main claim to fame on the field is the ability to use their extra height in *line-outs*.

A line-out is a set piece of play where the ball is thrown by the hooker from the sideline towards the two rows of forwards. Obviously a tall second row forward will be best placed to catch the ball. It is this height differential that also gives lock forwards their other reputation – that of being highly sociable.

Their ability to catch a barmaid's eye develops much earlier than their peers, as does their ability to hoodwink a barman into believing they are over the drinking age limit when in truth they still have a couple of years to go before reaching the officially sanctioned age for such pursuits.

They can thus be relied on to get in a round of drinks no matter who is paying – merely asking a pint as fee for this service. No wonder they have a reputation for joining in the end-of-match celebrations at the bar earlier than the rest of their team mates.

The Back Row Forwards

Not to be confused with the backs, the back row forwards are made up of the Number 8 and two flankers or wing forwards at Numbers 6 and 7. The back row players are expected to use their brains as well as their brawn. The flankers are the enemies of the opposition half-backs, whose lives are under constant threat from their crunching tackles. There is a blindside flanker at Number 6 and an openside flanker at Number 7.

The position of the blindside flanker depends on the proximity of a *touch line*, so if the scrum takes place close to the left hand touch line, the blindside flanker will be closest to that touch line. If they are attacking or defending on the right hand side, the blindside flanker will switch to stand on the right hand side of the scrum. The openside flanker will line up on the side which has a wide open space ahead of him.

The Number 8 keeps the scrum together and controls the release of the ball once it has been heeled back through the legs of the scrum by the hooker – or at least that is the theory.

The back row forwards tend to be popular positions in the early stages of learning the game. Young players discover they don't like having someone else's head crammed up against their backsides and prefer standing at the back of the scrum.

Incidentally, flankers have a well-deserved reputation for being excellent blood donors. Sadly, little of this makes it as far as the national transfusion service, most being spilt over rugby shirts and fields. If play is stopped for an injury, it's a pretty good bet that the player on the floor will be a bleeding flanker – assuming the full back is not involved.

The Backs – their roles and play

Traditionally each player has a set number designating their role in the team. However, numbers worn by team members can vary these days, with some clubs using letters of the alphabet and senior players having squad numbers which greatly exceed 15. The diagram below shows the traditional way that backs would line up at the kick-off or behind the scrum, with the standard numbering associated with their positions. This group of players stands behind the forwards and they are expected to run towards their opposition or tackle them as required.

The backs consist of Number 9 or scrum-half, Number 10 the fly-half, Number 11 on the left wing, Number 12 the inside centre, Number 13 the outside centre and at Number 14 there's the right wing. Numbers 11, 12, 13 and 14 are also sometimes known as the three-quarter backs or three-quarters. Finally Number 15 is the full back.

The Half-backs

These are the fly-half (or Outside Half) at Number 10 and the scrum-half, at Number 9. You'll rapidly learn that both the scrum-half and the fly-half think they are in charge of the game/team tactics, which can make for interesting conflicts during the course of a game.

They care deeply about things like ball pressure (obviously a soft ball bounces less well than a well pumped-up ball). They discuss crosswinds and options, things the majority of the team couldn't give a toss about.

Generally they are regarded as more intelligent than their team mates and they are frequently expected to make end-of-season reports on behalf of their team at junior level. Rugby supporters, please see our useful score sheet at the back of this book which may help.

The Scrum-half

The main role of scrum-halves is to act as the link between the forwards and the backs. Of all the players on the pitch, the scrum-half probably does the most running about as he or she dashes from one situation to the next to link forwards and backs together. They are therefore particularly fit individuals in a rugby team.

The scrum-half is frequently the smallest person on the pitch. He's the one you see throwing the ball at the feet of the group hug and then dashing to the back of this group to pick the ball out again (which seems such a waste of time until you understand what's going on) in order to throw it back to the fly-half who may then pass it on to the three-quarters to run the ball.

This is often done with what looks like an attempt on his part to defy gravity and fly, which then leads to him landing flat on the ground in the mud whilst the forwards rampage over the top of him to get to the ball. Actually this is one of the funnier sights available to supporters watching a game - and generally the scrum-half survives unharmed despite the rampaging forwards. As a result of these plays they are generally the children with the most understanding mothers, as their kit will usually be the muddiest (except perhaps for the full back, of which more later).

As part of their role scrum-halves frequently kick the ball away from the opposition to gain territory. The ball can, for instance, be given a short, shallow kick forwards, bouncing it along the ground under the opponents' feet. This is known as a *grubber kick* and will force the opposition to stop and turn; they may find it more difficult to collect or gather the ball from the ground. In many ways this is the reverse of the *up and under* kick we describe later on. Alternatively the ball can be kicked up and over an opponent and then the player can dash after it and pick it up again. This is known as *chip and chase.*

A flying half-back

Another standard scrum-half kick is a *box kick* which goes backwards high over his shoulder while he is facing his own attacking team members. This is used in tight attacking or defensive situations and always surprises the opposition when the ball emerges from the scrum-half over his shoulder and they have to turn and chase it back down the pitch.

The Fly-half

Usually one of the quickest thinkers on the pitch, the fly-half is responsible for ultimately deciding whether it is worth running the ball - either individually or by passing it down the line of backs - or whether the team would get farther down the pitch if they kicked the ball towards the opposition and risked losing it to them.

As a result of these options fly-halves are frequently blamed for the ball being lost to the other team, and need great strength of character to withstand the complaints of their team mates when they get a decision wrong. Of course, when the decision goes well and the ball bounces neatly into touch to set up a line-out near the try line, they are everyone's hero.

Some fly-halves have self-belief beyond their skillset and can be seen dashing off with the ball, traversing the pitch at speed and confusing the opposition (and their team mates too occasionally). Their natural inclination to run with the ball being hard-wired, they sometimes do that over and over again until a series of tackles reminds them that they do have other options.

They are also fearsome tacklers themselves, despite their sometimes small stature in comparison to the forwards they glibly choose to tackle. Sadly this can result in injuries and wounded fly-halves abound at senior level. Jonny Wilkinson of England was a prime example, when, despite his brilliance he was frequently injured and unable to play. Happily at more junior levels injuries are rarer.

The Three-Quarter Backs (or just "the three-quarters")

These are the inside and outside centres and the two players on the wing – four players in all. We give details of their positions and roles on the following pages.

The Centres or Centre Three-Quarter Backs

The centres (Numbers 12 and 13) line up outside the fly-half and are next in line to receive the ball as it's being passed down the line of backs who are attacking the try line.

If the ball is being run well and there are not many members of the opposition team ahead of them, they will occasionally even pass it out to the wings, those speedy individuals (at junior level not always particularly large members of the team) who can be relied on to sprint for the line and score tries if they are not tackled first.

Centres are also aggressive tacklers and all opposition backs (and even some forwards) dread a tackle from these players. They have to use their intelligence to decide which way to pass the ball to avoid their team being tackled by the opposition which would result in them losing the ball.

One of them frequently looks upon himself as a *crash ball* specialist and will set up attacks by running straight at the opposition tacklers without any sign of fear for his own personal safety. The centres are also capable of giving their team mates passes which will clearly result in them getting tackled and indeed may result in their possible injury due to the number of opposition they face, rather than facing up to the tackle themselves. These are known as *hospital passes*.

Like their fly-half team-mates, they sometimes take a decision to dash off in the opposite direction across the pitch on receiving the ball. You'll rapidly discover that this bold manoeuvre, at least at junior level, invariably results in the centre running straight into the *pack* of opposition forwards, getting tackled and losing the ball, much to his team mates' disgust.

The Wingers (Wings or Wing Three-quarters)

The wings (Numbers 11 and 14) can end a game of rugby without ever touching the ball, thanks to a combination of the forwards not letting the backs see the ball in the first place, and the centres not wanting to pass the ball out to them but preferring to disappear off in the opposite direction across the pitch as I've described above.

Just occasionally though, little wings will get the chance to sprint all the way down the length of the pitch, skirting with the danger of the touch line, side-stepping and dodging their way around lumbering forwards and exhausted backs in the opposition, leaving them trailing in their wake until they eventually cross the try line and score that elusive prize – a try.

Cheers from the crowd are never more heartfelt than when one of these valuable little members of the team scores in this fashion.

Whilst junior wings are frequently small and speedy, the arrival of Jonah Lomu of New Zealand on the international scene towards the end of the 20th century changed that tendency for ever. Senior level players are now quite tall but still remain speedy individuals. Top flight Olympic sprinters are taller these days too – just a sign of the times perhaps.

So, wingers think of themselves as the sprinters of the rugby squad and spend hours running up and down the pitch, hardly ever touching the ball. By the time players reach senior level their patience has generally run out, and they may track across the pitch to ensure they get to receive the passed ball at least once in a match. However at junior level such independence is frowned upon, as part of their role is defensive and moving from their allotted side of the pitch could result in the opposition scoring a try without being tackled.

Given how cold they can get, just standing around waiting for the rugby ball to reach them, it's a miracle they can actually catch it and run from a standing start to score tries. If your offspring is a wing you'll always get to see plenty of them, as you can usually stand on the touch line next to them throughout the match. Do try however not to distract them by offering sustenance or warm drinks during a game, however tempting that might seem. They will thaw out later.

The Full Back

Finally we come to the full back, the Number 15 in the team, who seemingly enjoys getting stamped all over by the opposition when cleanly catching high balls. He will bounce up from the heap of players, waving away any trainer who might want to treat any wounds sustained in the process, then having cleared the ball by kicking it back down the pitch, he will search the skies again for the next high ball to catch.

Full backs really hope this will give them a chance to run back at the opposition, despite the high risk of being trampled under foot yet again as the attacking team chases after the ball but this option rarely happens.

If your offspring frequently returns from rugby practices or matches claiming that the rest of the team have blamed them for losing the match, it is a pretty certain bet that he or she is a full back. As the last line of defence for the team, if all the others have failed to stop a marauding attack from the opposition, they can be relied upon to throw themselves selflessly at the feet of the thundering attacker in a desperate attempt to halt the opposition's progress towards the try line.

All too frequently they will fail, as their opposite number is likely to be (a) heavier, (b) taller and (c) coming towards them at great speed.

On a good day however they can kick the ball long and hard to get their team out of trouble and halt that attack. Sometimes they even set up good running tries with the careful placement of a kick that a winger can chase down, catch and then run with the ball to score at the opposite end of the pitch. Because of their long-kicking ability, the full back can also take the *conversion kicks* and *penalty kicks* – although this role is frequently shared with the fly-half.

However, there is another reason for a youngster becoming a full back. During those first lessons at school or first practices at a rugby club, they may conclude that this position right at the back of the team (somewhat similar to a goal keeper in Association Football) affords the best position from which to avoid any action whatsoever and keep them from getting hurt. They will eventually learn that this is definitely not the case, but for a brief period of time will enjoy playing rugby without any contact – indeed, they may hardly touch the ball or the opposition at all.

So now they have a position, what happens next?

Initially younger players will learn to pass the ball from hand to hand and will play *touch* or *tag rugby*, also known as *mini rugby* at rugby clubs and schools where youngsters can start to learn the game.

You will find more information on tag and mini rugby at: http://www.rfu.com/ManagingRugby/ClubDevelopment/Players/MiniAndYouth and http://www.internationalminirugby.com, and http://www.rfu.com/thegame/formsofrugby/tag

For worried parents, touch rugby merely means that small children will not be learning how to tackle (or bring down) their opponents just yet, but will just touch them lightly with a hand in order to trigger the passing of the ball to another player. Failing that, they have to hand the ball over to the opposition on instruction from the referee. Tag rugby involves a tag attached to a belt - a system we explain in the glossary.

However, touch rugby does not last for ever and before long they will be tackling their friends and crashing happily to the ground with them – in most homes this is known as the start of 'the washing season'.

Washing Season and Kit Purchase

Washing and cleaning tips

So your youngster has taken up playing rugby and guess what? They get muddy!

Once your young player has mastered tackling, your washing load will instantly increase as muddy rugby shorts, socks and shirts are brought home after every games lesson (and practice) and are needed, clean and pressed, frequently for the next day! The advantages of having a second string (or perhaps second-hand) set of kit clothing to save the panic washing and drying of kit will rapidly become apparent. Of course if you have children away at boarding school, then it is poor Matron and her team who will have to tackle the laundry - lucky you.

Rugby kit is specially designed to take rough treatment and responds well to all the standard biological and stain removing washing products available on the market. The joy of a combination of a good stain remover and a biological washing powder or liquid will usually guarantee clean kit for your keen rugby player, without too much effort on your part.

More old fashioned ways of keeping kit clean still work of course and these may be useful if your player has any skin problems that preclude biological products from being used or your waste water system doesn't allow you to use them.

These include soaking blood-stained items in strongly salted water overnight before washing. When most of the stain has gone, your can rub the residue with a paste of table salt mixed with a small amount of water. Soak the item in washing detergent for a few more hours, then wash as usual. You should be aware that you must never use hot water on blood stains (or wine stains for that matter) until the stain has gone or it will be sealed in permanently.

The traditional techniques for removing other stains include:

- Grass - sponge with warm soapy water and a little methylated spirit or eucalyptus oil.
- Mud - just soak first in cold water until dissolved then wash well.
- Perspiration - dissolve two aspirin tablets in water to remove stains, or mix a tablespoon (15 ml) of white vinegar in a third of a pint (200 ml) of water and sponge the affected area, then soak in detergent, then wash as normal.

If these more labour intensive methods don't appeal, you can always use a biological cleaner first as a prewash and then wash again, in non-biological products.

Of course some boys seem able to play in mud-caked and hardened kit from day to day without ever bringing it home, but the school teachers and club coaches soon put a stop to this and will suggest that getting their kit added to the family washing load is greatly preferable to gassing the rest of the team.

If you are lucky (and the teachers/coaches continue to hold sway) your small son or daughter will have a shower after each rugby training session and then at least they will return home fairly clean. If you are not so lucky, they will change rapidly into their school uniform or casual clothing before anyone notices they haven't showered and you may catch them scratching the mud off their legs whilst trying to do homework, watching television or playing computer games later in the day.

At this stage we suggest you insist that they show you their mud-covered limbs and then force them into the bathroom as quickly as possible. The earlier you can catch them, the less fine mud dust will be found on the carpet the next morning!

We imagine this is not generally a problem girls will present to their parents, but forewarned is forearmed.

Kit purchase

Kit is supplied from various sources including online suppliers. At school, the school's own sports shop may supply kit at reasonable prices, or the local school uniform shop may be another source. As previously mentioned, you should bear in mind that you will need at least two sets of kit, as sports masters have a habit of planning practice sessions just before matches against other schools when your son or daughter will then be expected to turn up in pristine kit to meet their opposition.

At public schools pupils will also need house colour rugby shirts as well as school shirts but it's well worth checking if your school or club has a second hand shop. It's not a cheap thing this kit lark, and that's without even starting on rugby boots.

Boots

Rugby boots have changed considerably in the past few decades and are generally interchangeable with football boots these days. However, players **must** change the studs to the safe version specifically designed for use in rugby. These studs are designed to grip the surface of the pitch without injuring other players when they come in close proximity during play. If traditional football boot studs are retained they could cause untold damage to fellow players in a ruck or maul situation.

Studs come in two lengths to allow for both muddy and dry grassy conditions and need to be changed before a match depending on the state of the pitch. In the end most players play in the shorter studs most of the time as they find it difficult to run in the longer studs anyway. Some football boots come fitted with blades instead of studs but these are not at all appropriate for rugby, because they don't give enough traction on a muddy pitch.

Headgear

Headgear has also changed greatly in recent years and many young players are now encouraged to wear scrum caps previously only worn by one or two members of the scrum front and second rows. Anxious mothers will be pleased to learn that this protective headgear has become acceptable to all and players are considered wise rather than wimpish if they sport them. However learning to tackle without protection will ensure safe tackling skills are learned from an early age.

Body armour

Although padded undershirts are often used at senior level to protect shoulders from damage in the tackle and scrum they are very much discouraged for junior players. It is really not sensible to encourage your youngster to use such items until they are secure in tackling without them - they are far less likely to tackle too hard without added protection than with it. Senior players are getting injured these days because they think their padded shoulders and scrum caps will protect them, and it's very important that junior players don't adopt these protective devices too soon. Tackling safely is always possible when a player knows his limitations, and any protection that lessens a sense of self-preservation should be avoided.

Protection for the teeth

Mouthguards, or gum shields, of course, are essential. Schools and clubs advise proper fitting by a dentist, with adjustments before each season, to avoid unnecessary mouth injuries and discomfort from ill-fitting 'ready-made' products. Your young player will be pleased to know that dentists are well aware of the need for style in a mouthguard, and for a reasonable sum your young player can wear a smile to frighten the boldest forward in the opposition.

Personally, I was always particularly fond of the single white tooth in the middle of a black mouthguard - it's always amusing for the spectators.

The final article of clothing, a total mystery to most women but an essential piece of sports kit for the men in their lives, is the athletic support, or jock strap. This flimsy contraption is designed to maintain equilibrium for the more sensitive parts of the male anatomy, and is worn under the shorts.

The first visit to a sports supplier to purchase this particular piece of kit is something that may well be better left to a father, uncle or grandfather, but all too frequently this task will fall to a mother. Thankfully, these days, the advent of slip underwear and fitted boxer shorts means the need to wear an athletic support is less essential for youngsters, but it's worth bearing in mind that this might be something you get asked for and we hope that knowledge of its existence may (if nothing else) minimise the embarrassment for both parties.

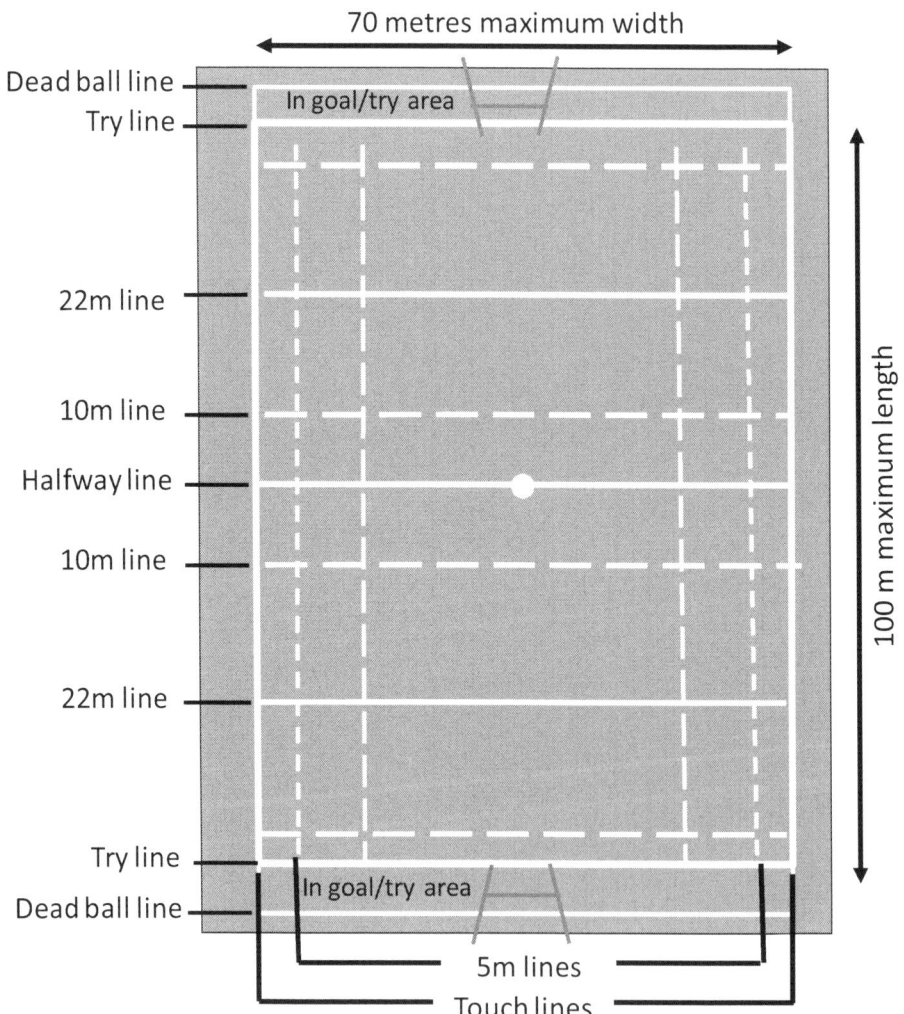

The Game

We hope you are beginning to have a feel for what Rugby Union is all about, so it is time to have a go at describing the game itself. Just to make things easy let's start by describing the ground on which it is played – the pitch.

The Pitch

Rugby is played on a field up to 100 metres (330 ft) long and 70 metres (230 ft) wide with H-shaped goal posts on each goal line. You can see what a rugby pitch looks like from a bird's eye view in the diagram opposite.

The pitch is divided into several sections. At each end there is a section behind the goal posts marked by a white line. Between the edge of the pitch, on the goal line and level with the posts, and through to this white line is where a try can be scored. This is also known as the *in goal* or *try area*. The goal line can also be called the *try line* and the line behind the posts called the *dead ball line*. If the ball keeps on travelling until it passes the dead ball line it is no longer in play. No one can score by touching it down once it has passed that line, and it will be returned to the 22-metre line for a *drop-out* kick by the defending team. If a defender kicks or takes the ball over the dead ball line this will result in a 5-metre scrum.

In addition to the try area, the pitch is also marked with a centre or halfway line and a spot through which the starting *kick-off* is taken. Other lines marked on the pitch include 22-metre lines and 10-metre lines and along the length of the pitch there are lines marked at 5 and 15 metres into the pitch. The touch lines are the lines down the sides of the pitch; line-outs take place here when the ball has been kicked or knocked into touch. But more importantly this is where you will be standing as a spectator.

Supporters stand on or next to the touch lines during a game to cheer on their team. Depending on your child's or partner's position, you may choose to stand at a particular point on the touch line in order to see as much as possible of them as they play in a game.

Of course if the player you've come to watch is the scrum-half you're going to get a lot of exercise - you'll be dashing from one end of the pitch to the other to keep track of the action. Not only is the scrum-half the fittest player on the pitch, his supporters will need to be pretty fit as well.

Playing a Game

Games are played in two halves of 40 minutes, with a short break at half time when teams swop ends for the second half of the match, sometimes taking time for refreshments and clean shirts and shorts depending on the weather.

Referees keep strict time records, stopping their watches when play halts, for whatever reason, to ensure exactly 40 minutes of actual play takes place in each half.

As we explained earlier, when playing rugby, the first and most important rule or Law to learn is that the ball may only be passed laterally or backwards, never forwards towards the opposing team's goal line.

In fact, the ball can only be moved forwards in three ways: (1) by kicking it, (2) by a player running holding onto it or (3) within a scrum, ruck or maul.

Only the player with the ball may be tackled or rucked and defenders cannot tackle or even block any other players. Blocking or tripping is a foul called *obstruction* that gets penalised by the referee.

When a ball is knocked forwards to the ground by players using their arms or hands, a *knock-on* is committed, and play is restarted with a scrum. All players are allowed to kick the ball forwards in an attempt to gain territory and we give full details of this type of play later in this book.

Every game starts with a kick-off where a *drop kick* is used from the centre of the halfway line to start the match. The ball must travel at least 10 metres away from the kick off point towards the opposition goal line before it hits the ground for this kick to be within the Laws, and if this doesn't happen it is penalised with a scrum. It's obviously helpful that the 10 metre lines are marked on the pitch. If the ball goes the correct distance and is picked up by either the attacking or defending team it can then be passed between them, and this is known as *open play*.

Once a young player has mastered the basic rules of passing and tackling (of which more later) the more complicated rules and regulations will start to enter into their skills.

Touching Down – Scoring a Touch Down or Try

In order to touch the ball down and score a try, the player carrying the ball merely has to push it down on the grass inside the in-goal area over the try line. They can also do this by diving towards the ground with the ball safely in their hands.

In recent years a young England rugby winger called Chris Ashton has developed something of a reputation for scoring in this way (not unlike our flying half-back on page 19). Alternatively, if the ball has been kicked over the goal line, players can race and dive after it to slap the ball down with either one or both hands.

The vision of a speeding half-back racing over the line and launching himself at the ball is another of the funny sights available to watching parents, perhaps only bettered by the sight of a scrum-half trying to peer over the shoulders or through the legs of a particularly large second-row or back-row forward to see where the ball has gone in a scrum or a line-out.

The most important aspect of try scoring is that the scorer must use downward pressure on the ball as it hits the ground over the try line, or the try won't count. Television replays of tries frequently spend many minutes trying to establish if downward pressure has been put on the ball before a try is allowed.

Tackling skills

Players are only allowed to tackle an opposing player who is holding the ball (known as the ball carrier). They do this by holding onto them while bringing them down to the ground, i.e. one or two knees are on the ground or they are sitting on the ground or even on top of another player who is on the ground.

Tacklers cannot tackle above their opponent's shoulder line (the neck and head are considered out of bounds), and tacklers have to attempt to wrap their arms around the player being tackled to complete the tackle. It is illegal to push, shoulder-charge, or to trip a player using feet or legs, but hands may be used (this is referred to as a *tap-tackle* or *ankle-tap*).

The standard tackle involves one player grasping another around or below the waist to pull their opponent to the ground. Shirts are sometimes torn at junior levels of rugby as shirt grabbing is easier to manage when players are first learning how to tackle. Tackles made above the shoulder are termed *high tackles* and these are penalised by the referee offering a penalty kick to the opposition.

Players will soon discover that while grabbing a shirt may help to topple a slight running back, it will rarely have any effect on the more robust and sturdy forwards.

Swinging players around by the arm can also be effective when size and weight differences are greater in young players moving into their early teenage years, but this is obviously discouraged. Some youngsters mature faster than others and this makes size differences quite noticeable. Ideally, however, all tackles should take place around the waist or below.

The Tap Tackle

This is a perfectly legal means of tackling a running player, by tapping the back of their feet or legs whilst they are running to upset their balance and trip them up. The runner is less likely to get hurt than the tackler, however, who risks being kicked in the face as he or she reaches for the speeding player's heels. Many full backs are masters of this masochistic form of tackling and proudly sport the resultant black eyes.

Kicking the ball

Whilst the ball is traditionally carried in rugby, as we've already explained it is also kicked in several situations, especially by the scrum-half.

(1) Conversion kicks

When a try has been scored, the team's best kicker (usually the fly-half or full back) will try to convert that try by kicking the ball over the crossbar and between the posts. The ball is always placed back on the pitch exactly in line with the point where the try was scored, but the kicker can move as far backwards (away from the goal) as they want, before taking the kick. If the try is scored near the touch line, for instance, the kicker usually goes back a good distance to widen the angle of the kick in order to score. If the try is scored underneath the posts, kickers will only go back a few metres to allow themselves an easy kick to score the conversion.

(2) Penalty kicks

These are taken whenever the opposition has broken the Laws in some way (see infringements later). The kick is taken through the point where the infringement occurred and can either be taken by the ball being placed on the ground and kicked, or by the kicker holding it in his hands and dropping the ball to kick it in the air after it has hit the ground. This is a known as a *punt*.

Penalty kicks taken in front of the goal posts can result in points being scored if the ball succeeds in passing through the posts in the required manner. Some senior players have the ability to kick penalty goals from behind the half-way line, but they are a rare breed. In Europe Jonny Wilkinson of England and Chris Patterson of Scotland both became famous for their unerring ability with conversions, drop goals and penalty kicks. In Jonny's case this included his dramatic last minute drop goal which won the Rugby World Cup for England in 2003, which you can see on this link:

http://www.youtube.com/watch?v=-m-0v8KlNoA&feature=fvwrel

(3) Clearance kicks

These can be taken at any time during the game and are normally used to improve a side's position on the pitch. These include the grubber kick and box kick that we described earlier as being used by the scrum-half as a regular part of his play. As long as the ball bounces in the field of play before going into touch, a throw-in is taken by a member of the opposition team at the point where the ball crosses the touch line. Players quick off the mark can throw the ball in to their team mates before the opposition arrives to force a line-out, but usually such kicks will result in a line-out being taken.

In addition, if a player is standing inside his own 22-metre area and kicks directly into touch (i.e. without the ball bouncing in-field first), a line-out will be taken by the opposition where the ball went into touch. However if the ball is kicked into touch directly by a player standing outside his team 22-metre area, or if his team-mates have carried or passed the ball back into that area just prior to the kick being taken, then the line-out is taken level to where the kick was made.

(4) **Very high (clearance) kicks**

These are used to help the attacking team move towards the try line in the hope that their team mates will catch the ball or at least compete for it. These are the kicks nicknamed 'up-and-unders' in Rugby League football and 'Garryowens' in Union. Some people think this name was after the Limerick Rugby Union club that used the technique so much during its games the name stuck. Others say the kick was named after Garfield Owen, a famous Welsh fullback from the 1950s who was renowned for using the technique. Whichever way it started, it's a common term that's good to know about if you hear it on a TV or radio commentary.

It might seem that the backs are giving the ball to the opposition by doing this, but the poor young player trying to catch the swirling ball as it plummets towards him from high in the sky, whilst a horde of speeding backs and enormous forwards charge towards him, stands little chance of catching it cleanly. Actually, the attacking team frequently goes on to pick up the ball and run with it again. Of course it is traditional for full backs to be the defending catchers – no wonder they live in fear of their team mates blaming them for losing the game.

Forward Play

For the forwards (or the pack as they are sometimes called) this will include line-outs, mauls and rucks as well as scrums. The main role of the forwards is to wrest the ball from the opposition through these various modes of play. If a ball goes off the side of the pitch (i.e. over the touch line) a line-out will be taken.

Line-outs

Many disagreements will occur at the start of a line-out since it is never the team that kicked, threw or dropped the ball over the touch line that gets to throw it back in, it is always their opposition (exactly as in Association Football). A ball can, of course, be accidentally touched by opposition players after a kick is taken, before it crosses the touch line, and this often results in disagreements as to whose throw-in it is going to be.

However, once it has been established which team is taking the throw-in, which in a match will be clearly shown by the referee's colleagues (the touch judges), it is the job of that team's hooker to throw the ball, straight, over the heads of and between the two rows of forwards. One of them will jump up and catch or use his hand(s) to push the ball back towards his team mates (especially the backs), who are all lined up waiting for the ball to emerge.

The forwards from each team must stand in line behind each other in two straight lines about one metre apart. This gap must be maintained until the ball is thrown in, and teams can be penalised for not maintaining the gap. The opposition hooker normally stands next to the throwing hooker until the ball has been thrown.

A regular line-out will have all the forwards in the lines (except the hookers of course). A short line-out can reduce that number to as few as two in each line but this rarely happens.

Sometimes a shortened line-out is used to allow the hooker to throw the ball right over the forward lines and link up with another fast-moving forward, or, more generally, a speeding back who will catch the ball and charge off with it towards the try line.

The attacking team uses secret codes to confirm which player will be catching the ball and strange shouts of 'Himalayas' or codes like '137' can be heard being yelled over the line of forwards before the hooker throws the ball. This gives the attacking team an advantage at the start of the match, but oppositions frequently work out what the codes mean and are able to contest effectively for the ball soon after a game commences.

Once the ball has been thrown by the hooker, the forwards usually help one of their number to leap in the air to catch it as it passes over and between their heads. Generally a second row lock forward (if you remember, likely to be one of the tallest members of the team) is helped up into the air by two of his team mates and ideally catches the ball, landing back on the ground clutching it to his chest. If he catches the ball safely, he then turns his back on the opposition to set up a maul or a ruck (we'll explain the difference between these later) until the ball emerges from the back of the forwards group to be passed back to the scrum-half.

It's important to know that no player who jumps for the ball in a line-out is allowed to be tackled until they are safely down on the ground again. Line-outs are frequently turned into penalty kicks when the jumping player is pulled, held, shoved or leant on by his opposite number before his feet have touched the ground again.

If the leaping forwards are unable to take the ball cleanly from the hooker's throw, they can tap the ball down towards a receiver, a player who stands next to the line-out to wait for such a pass, usually the scrum-half. However, if they do this they are only allowed to use either their inside arm/hand or both arms/hands, never their outside arm alone.

Once the receiver has the ball he will hopefully pass it out to the fly-half who will then pass it on to the other backs for them to run the ball, or he may kick the ball as far as possible down the pitch to gain territory (a clearance kick). This is generally an unpopular move with supporters as it frequently results in possession of the ball transferring to the opposition.

The line-out is the part of the game where many infringements can occur (including pushing, closing the gap etc.). If, after an attempted line-out, the ball is immediately handed to the other team to kick, you can guarantee that the team you're supporting has committed one of these infringements.

Another minor infringement in the line-out, which would result in a scrum being taken, could be a knock-on (where, you may remember, a player drops or knocks the ball forwards onto the ground with hands or arms). You will notice that knock-ons also occur when backs are running with the ball and passing it to another player who does not quite catch the ball but drops it forwards.

If the hooker is asked to throw the ball again, it may be that they did not manage to throw the ball in straight between and over the lines of forwards. When your youngster is still learning the game, school and club referees will frequently let them have a second go. Once the rules have been learned, however, this would be penalised and the opposition would be offered the choice of a scrum or another line-out, and this time their hooker will get to throw or put the ball in.

The final way a hooker can throw the ball in, is to pass it straight to the first forward in the line – this is most frequently done at shortened line-outs. If the line-out is taking place close to the try line, this can result in the forward catching the ball and launching himself over the line to score a try, much to the amazement of the opposition players. However, the ball must always travel at least five metres from the hooker before it is touched by another player. Quick throw-ins are sometimes taken but fail to travel far enough and this results in the ball being lost to the opposition.

Scrums

No they're not just a team bonding exercise or group hug as they may seem, scrums are used as a way of restarting the game when the ball has gone out of play, either when the ball becomes unplayable in a ruck or maul (explained later) or following a minor infringement of the Laws. The scrum (or scrummage) consists of the three rows of forward players from each team, and the front row (tight-head prop, hooker and loose-head prop) will *engage* with the front row of the opposition, so that their heads interlock, forming a kind of *tunnel* between heads and feet. This is where you will realise the tight-head and loose-head prop names have a reason; the tight-head prop ends up with his head enclosed on both sides by opposition heads, while the loose-head prop only has one side of his head against the opposition.

The ball is placed in the centre of the tunnel by the scrum-half, and the two packs compete for the ball by trying to hook the ball backwards with their feet and kick it out to one of the other players waiting on the field. A scrum often occurs after a foul has taken place (this can be anything from a knock-on, or crooked throw-in, to accidental offside) and it can be an alternative to a free kick.

All the backs, except the scrum-half, retreat away from the position of the scrum and, from the new supporter's view, they seem to pretty much leave the forwards to get on with it. The ball is then thrown into the middle of the gap (or tunnel) between the two teams by the scrum-half and both sides must compete to try and hook the ball and send it backwards through the scrum with their feet. During the scrum, both sets of forwards push against their opposition in an attempt to gain possession of the ball. You will hear television and radio commentators referring to this as 'contesting the scrum'.

Once possession of the ball has been secured, a team can keep the ball on the ground and inside the scrum and attempt to drive the opposition backwards down the field. Once the ball reaches the hindmost foot in the scrum (normally the Number 8's foot), the ball can be picked up and carried forward or passed.

This is where the scrum-half is a key player – being responsible for putting the ball in and frequently for picking it out of the back of the scrum. You should be aware that once the ball is picked up the forwards are allowed to let go of each other and tackle their opposition. You will frequently hear a shout of 'out' when the scrum-half lets his team know they can unbind because the ball is back in open play.

The forwards line up as shown on the next page. As we've already explained, most rugby shirts are numbered to tally with the positions on the field and in the scrum – like this diagram. The Loose-head prop (1) will always stand on the left hand side of his team, the Tight-head prop (3) is on the right. However with senior teams playing squad members in rotation these days, sadly you can no longer guarantee that the man wearing Number 9 is the scrum-half or the Number 8 shirt wearer is necessarily the back row man. However at true amateur level the numbers still remain constant and you should be able to work out where a player should be on the pitch by checking their shirt number.

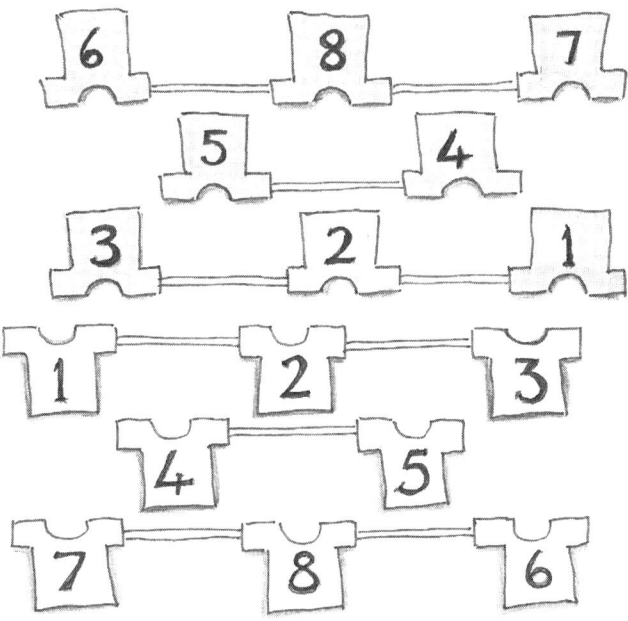

If this really interests you, there is more information on scrummaging skills at the following websites:

www.irb.com

http://www.talkrugbyunion.co.uk/

or from

http://www.rugby-sidestep-central.com/rugby-positions.html

A word of warning; if your tall son or daughter asks you for a bandage and sticky tape to tape their ears down before playing rugby, please don't be surprised. The discomfort they could incur as fellow forwards hug them, crushing their hips against their heads, or alternatively as they crush their own heads against the opposition's heads as the scrum comes together, will rapidly convince you that taping down their ears is the least of their problems. It should be noted however that most youthful forwards are not generally masochistic enough to do this and only the toughest amongst these young players will take to taping their ears from an early age, especially as there now excellent scrum caps - IRB approved head gear - that players have taken to wearing if they are in those difficult positions in the scrum, but see our caution on their use on page 29.

See http://www.irbplayerwelfare.com/?documentid=52

As a point of curiosity, the scrummage was adopted under its old name of scrimmage by the Americans to form a permanent part of their version of football. The word fell out of favour for Rugby Union, but remains in use in the USA.

What really happens in a Scrum?

We've already given you a basic idea but here's the detail on what goes on in the group hug known as a scrum. The scrum-half who is about to place or throw the ball into the scrum stands to the left of his own hooker with the opposition scrum-half standing next to him on the same end of the pitch as the rest of his team.

Once the scrum has formed on both sides, the forwards all brace themselves and wait for the instructions from the referee to 'crouch' [the individual packs bind together linking arms and crouch down], 'touch' [the props on each side touch each other's shoulders to demonstrate they are standing close enough to meet in the middle on the final command], 'hold' [the two packs hold steady – steeling themselves for the next move] and 'engage'. With each of these commands they move closer together, and finally the front rows link up on the word 'engage'.

The ball is then thrown into the middle of the gap between the two front rows (*putting-in* to the tunnel) and the two hookers compete for possession of the ball, with the entire pack jostling and pushing against each other to make the task of hooking even more difficult. The hookers are both trying to hook the ball backwards with a foot or leg towards their own team. The packs push against each other, sometimes twisting the scrum around in their effort.

Gradually one side will get the ball to the back of the scrum, where the little scrum-half will have dashed – standing just behind the rearmost foot of the back row forwards in the scrum. Here he will dice with death again and pick the ball up once more (not an easy act for a little person surrounded by enormous forwards as we've previously said) and then pass it to the other backs, usually via the fly-half. It is commonplace for the team that throws the ball into the scrum to retain possession of it, as the scrum-half and hooker can synchronise their actions so the latter knows when to strike to hook the ball back into the scrum. In addition, particularly at junior level, right-footed hookers will find it easier to hook with their right foot as the ball comes into the tunnel towards the attacking team's players.

However, this is not guaranteed. If a scrum twists too far around (known as *wheeling the scrum*) the referee will blow his whistle and make the packs re-set and start the process all over again. If he considers one team is causing the wheeling round deliberately, he will penalise them.

If the forwards all fall over on top of each other, this is called a *collapsed scrum* and if it is obviously accidental the same scrum-half will get the chance to put in a second time, once all the forwards have stood up and reorganised themselves into a new scrum.

If, however, the referee considers that one team deliberately brought down the scrum, then he will give the ball to the opposition team to take a penalty kick. In addition, the ball can be given to the opposition if the ball does not go straight into the tunnel (a Law that seems to be ignored quite a lot at more senior levels if the scrum-halves think the referee can't see their actions very clearly). The opposition will also be given the ball if the referee believes the scrum-half is holding onto the ball for too long before putting it into the scrum. Yes, being a scrum-half is a job full of responsibility – you can be justly proud of your offspring or partner if they play in this key position on the pitch.

Mauls and Rucks

More supporters new to the game of rugby ask: 'What's the difference between a maul and a ruck?', than almost any other question about rugby, especially when their youngsters are first learning the game.

So here goes with our simplified explanation: a *maul* occurs after a player holding the ball has come into contact with a tackler but remains on his or her feet. Once at least three players join or bind with the two original players, with the ball OFF the ground, a maul is formed and players in possession will try to pass it between each other as they move forwards towards the opposition try line. Sometimes they will choose to pass it back out to the backs to let them run with the ball and the maul breaks up. A rolling maul occurs when the forwards move out and round as the ball is passed back through the maul. They peel off at the front and side and rejoin the maul at the back, gaining territory and gradually moving forwards down the pitch towards the try line with the ball in hand. Generally the ball is kept near the rear of the maul so if progress gets halted by the opposition forwards, the ball can be easily passed out to the scrum-half for onward transmission to the backs.

That's a ruck . . . oh no it's a maul . . . well maybe it's a ruck

A *ruck* occurs when the same group hug seems to be taking place, but now the ball is down ON the ground. Once three players have joined the huddle after a tackle has taken place, a ruck will be formed with the ball at their feet (and sometimes the original ball carrier and his tackler too - it's not a pleasant place to be). The two teams of forwards push against each other (much as they do in a scrum) to push their own team over the ball until it reappears at the rear of the rucking players, whereupon either the scrum-half (lucky little person) can pick it up and pass it out to the backs, or the final forward (usually the Number 8) can pick the ball up and start to run forwards with it again.

You should note that the ball can be dropped to the ground in a maul (converting a maul to a ruck) as long as the ball is placed away from the line of play, in other words towards team mates and away from the opposition (otherwise, of course, it would count as a forward pass or knock-on). The other significant distinguishing feature is that no player can touch the ball with their hand inside a ruck, only feet can be used, until the ball reaches the back foot of the ruck, whereupon that forward only or the scrum-half can pick it up as described above.

Rugby games are frequently spent with the forwards moving from maul to ruck to maul and the backs may complain that they never get to see the ball, let alone run with it. Equally the forwards will complain back that when they do pass the ball to the backs the latter promptly lose it to the opposition and the forwards then have to go and get it back again.

New rules relating to rucks and mauls seem to come into effect from season to season, so do check with your youngster if you can't understand what's happening or check the IRB website www.irblaws.com for the latest instructions. http://www.rugby-sidestep-central.com is also very helpful in giving the layman or woman an idea of current thoughts on these aspects of playing rugby.

Number 8s are obviously key players in the forward pack at these set piece plays. They decide whether to continue pushing forward in a ruck or whether to try to run the ball again and try to progress with another maul or ruck if they get tackled. At scrums they use their feet to keep the ball inside the scrum so the opposition pack have to remain bound together, and the opposition scrum-half can't touch the ball until it comes out from the scrum. So it's quite important that the scrum-half and Number 8 get on well – they spend an awful lot of the match standing very close to each other and making vital decisions on behalf of their team mates. Because of their tactical skills and sheer size Number 8s are frequently appointed as team captain, and they command respect from both forwards and backs in equal measure.

Infringements (various) including dangerous play

The high tackle

You can regularly hear rugby commentators on television point out the dubious value of the high tackle. It flattens the best player in the opposition and can prevent him from taking any further part in the game. It is, of course, completely illegal and, thankfully all junior coaches and referees actively discourage its use, severely punishing any player who attempts it by removing them from the pitch – sometimes for the remainder of the game or even longer. Players have been banned for following games or even to the end of a season for dangerous high tackles.

A high tackle is one where the player grabs at their opponent's shoulders, neck or head, instead of grasping at their body around or below the waist. At junior level tall players will complain that it is difficult to get down low enough to tackle smaller players, but they too have to learn that a high tackle is potentially lethal.

Grabbing players by the collars of their shirts is similarly discouraged, and can be penalised by a penalty kick being given to the opposition. Again in severe cases, the offender will be sent off the pitch. At senior level this can be for a 10 minute *sin bin* wait on the touch line, indicated by the referee showing a yellow card, but they can also be sent off, or red-carded, just like Association Football players. They take no further part in the game if the tackle is considered sufficiently dangerous.

The (accidental) forward pass

As you now know, all passes which do not go laterally or behind the ball carrier are called forward passes and are illegal in rugby. They result in the ball being handed to the opposition for a scrum. All players will tell you that such passes are accidental, and indeed for juniors, given their level of competence, this will actually probably be true.

The hand-off

This is a useful weapon in the armoury of the more experienced rugby players. It consists of running with the ball tucked under one arm whilst holding the other arm out to the side, so that any unsuspecting opposition tackler will be pushed out of the way by the force of the oncoming player's hand and arm. This can be likened to jousting, where the lance was held out in the front of the rider so that he could topple his opponent by galloping at speed towards him.

It is a perfectly legal way of resisting being tackled but only with a bent arm and to the side of the player. 'Jousting' as such is not legal. It has a great psychological effect on the opposition once it is perfected. The sight of a large forward (or even a back) charging at you with his arm outstretched is surely enough to put fear into the bravest of little souls. The thought of having your shoulder pummelled by this speeding ramrod must be terrifying when it is first encountered.

Of course, the hand-off should only ever be aimed at the opponent's body, never their face, and it is an important technique to learn to use with care. Those who attack the opposition above the shoulder can be accused of high tackles which will always result in a penalty being awarded.

Pulling down the scrum

Scrums can and do collapse. The group hug can rapidly turn into what seems to be a group orgy (frequently punctuated with loud shouts of 'watch where you're stamping' and 'mind my head'). Usually the collapse is unintentional but occasionally it is deliberate.

This is, of course, a practice which should be severely discouraged from the earliest days, since it can result in very serious back and neck injuries to the forwards, and all players should be taught that it is illegal. If a referee believes the scrum has been deliberately brought down, he will penalise the team involved by offering their opposition a penalty kick. The referee demonstrates this by a double victory salute with both arms bent and clenched fists towards him which he pulls down in a move not too dissimilar to a dance move much beloved by bad-dancing dads.

All forwards should be taught that the aim of scrummaging is to push forwards against your opponents to push them up and back away from the ball and enable the ball to be heeled back to their own team's scrum-half. Once good practice has been absorbed it will hopefully never be forgotten and less dangerous play will safeguard all players' future rugby careers.

Holding onto the ball

When tackled and brought down to the ground, the ball must be released immediately (either by passing it whilst being tackled or by placing it on the ground). If the ball is not released, the team is penalised with a penalty kick being given to the opposition. The referee can be seen hugging himself to demonstrate that the offending player was holding onto the ball.

Offside

Rugby's offside law restricts where on the field players can be at any time to ensure there is space to attack and defend. A player is generally in an offside position if he or she is further forward than the ball carrier or the team mate who last played the ball. Whilst being in an offside position is not, in itself, an offence, any player who finds themselves offside should not take part in the game until they get themselves onside again. Of course, if they do touch the ball, they will be penalised.

Foul play in general

Any foul play should be discouraged, and the final lesson for all rugby players to learn is to control their tempers at all times – no matter how much they believe they have been provoked. If they can learn to control their own tempers, fewer injuries and penalties will occur. It's a good life lesson for them all.

The sin bin?

Advantage being played after an infringement

Sometimes during a game an infringement occurs where a stoppage in play would deprive the team that did not offend of an opportunity to score. Under these circumstances the Laws state that even though they should be awarded a penalty, free kick or scrum, they are given an opportunity to continue to play and attempt to score a try (assuming of course they retain control of the ball).

New supporters are frequently confused when an obvious infringement takes place, but play continues and then some time later the referee blows his whistle and takes the players back to the place where the first infringement happened for the penalty.

It can sometimes seem a very long time has elapsed between the original foul and the penalty being awarded, but if this happens the referee will have been applying the Law of *advantage* to give the attacking team a chance to score. If they are unable to do so, as long as only a relatively short period of time has elapsed, the referee can choose to return to the original infringement and award the penalty.

Supporters will see that throughout this advantage period the referee will hold his arm out to indicate he is playing advantage. Once his arm drops to his side and/or he calls out 'advantage over', the advantage period has ceased. Whatever happens next, the team originally given the advantage with the ball will no longer get the penalty that might previously have been awarded. That penalty has timed out.

Teams playing advantage can therefore take risky decisions in the full knowledge that if they don't work out, they will get to return to the site of the penalty and get advantage that way. For instance, this is the time when risky drop kicks at goal get taken. The lucky team is often able to take full advantage and score a try from such situations, so this Law can be very influential in the final result of a match.

Injuries and Protective Clothing

The leaders of the game are very aware of the potential for injury in this fast and furious contact sport. The Laws are regularly updated to ensure such injuries are kept to a minimum, but an occasional black eye will still occur (and indeed at junior level it is worn with some pride by the owner). Safety equipment has increased in the past decade, and as well as the traditional mouthguard (best obtained from your local dentist unless your child's club or school arranges special fitting sessions - see more information on page 30), padded undershirts with soft shoulder pads are now worn at senior level.

If a player is unfortunate enough to sustain an injury, it's always useful to know which local A&E department has the best reputation in these days of NHS cuts. Generally injuries will only be minor bumps and bruises and a hot bath and ice pack will resolve most of these relatively rapidly. Special medical ice packs are available but a bag of frozen peas wrapped in a tea towel will usually do the job cheaply and efficiently.

The importance of correct studs in playing boots will become very obvious the first time your child is stamped on and climbed over in a ruck or maul. With safety studs the resultant marks will be relatively minor and will heal rapidly. This would not be the case with standard football studs.

We all know the value of cold steak on a black eye, but there are alternatives: a traditional remedy is an application of a tincture of arnica, surgical spirit and water, or another of vinegar and water, but our favourite is witch-hazel liquid or gel, both readily available from your local pharmacy.

The following is an interesting combination recommended by Mrs Beeton of Household Management fame: 'chloride of ammonium (sal-ammoniac), 1 oz; rectified spirit, lavender water, or eau-de-Cologne, 2 oz; vinegar, 3 oz; water to make 16 ozs in all. Rags dipped in this solution should be laid over the bruise and kept constantly wet.' She notes that hot poultices are frequently more effective than cold applications in removing the associated discolouration. For this generation, a hot bath, an ice pack and some arnica and witch-hazel will usually do the trick.

It is also easy now to buy oral arnica and arnica cream as treatments for bruising and shock from your local chemist or health food shop. If your player gets cramp we recommend magnesium capsules. Magnesium sulphate paste works well on splinters and any gravel or grit embedded in knees or hands. We could go on, but you get the idea, most wounds are minor and just require basic first aid. Hopefully your child or partner will never experience a serious injury.

Learning how to lose gracefully

It is vital that all players learn that winning is not always possible and losing gracefully is a skill that all good sportsmen and women should embrace. You can encourage your young player to do this by not getting upset yourself when he loses. A supporter's role is more than patching up bodily injuries; boosting self confidence and morale through encouragement is also part of your role in endorsing the spirit of good sportsmanship.

Rugby Sevens

This version of rugby is generally played over 7 minutes each way, rather than the 80 minutes of a full side game, with just seven players on each side and 3 men per side in the scrum. Still under the Rugby Union banner, this version of the game uses the standard scoring system at senior level. Sevens is a faster, more try-friendly game with a shorter playing time and a tendency to have runaway results.

Sevens competitions at senior levels are also usually one or two-day affairs. Schools play in sevens competitions too and these are often all-day events that can be great fun to support.

Competitions take place all over the world at senior level with teams arranged in groups, points are awarded for wins and draws with group winners moving on to the next stage of the competition.

You can find out more on www.irb.com/sevens, http://www. rugbysevensguru.com/ and http://www.rfu.com/thegame/formsofrugby/ sevens

Rugby Tens also exists as a pre-season training game, with five forwards and five backs per team. Play is 10 minutes each way but includes full contact tackles. Pre-season Tens festivals now take place around the world and this is another great way to get into enjoying rugby as the games are shorter, but fast and furious and therefore great fun to watch.

Supporters' Etiquette

If you've ever been taken aback by the behaviour of rowdy football crowds, rest assured keen rugby supporters - especially parents - can be just as vociferous and ill-mannered. All schools ask their supporters to behave correctly at matches and some even issue their parents with guidelines, but this doesn't stop over-keen parents from screaming at their children mid-match entreating them to 'kill' the opposition. Obviously this is not acceptable. Good supporters should cheer both sides, although a certain degree of bias can be shown, naturally.

Well-behaved supporters will encourage their team, whilst applauding good play by the opposition, and without antagonising the match officials. They will also shout for the whole team without embarrassing individuals by shouting out their names. And of course once they understand a bit more about the game we hope they will **not** stand in a huddle just nattering to each other, ignoring the match itself and getting cold, but will finally actually enjoy following the match properly.

Final Thoughts

So there you have it. You know how many players are involved, what their positions and usual shirt numbers are, what is expected of them and how they play the game. You know pretty much everything you need to know to understand what's going on and what to expect yourself. You know the score in more ways than one.

Supporters are vitally important to the whole team, not just the individuals they come to watch. Cheers and encouragement make such a huge difference to the confidence of all the players, and can make a struggling team overcome superior opposition. Do have faith in your team - you never know what they are capable of unless you cheer them on.

And, of course, as you know, the supporters' role covers far more than valiant cheers at the touch line in all weathers - all the back-up work, kit preparation, safety equipment, the washing mountain, coping with injuries and defeats, helping with team teas . . . what would they do without you?

A SIMPLE GLOSSARY OF TERMS

advantage	A decision taken by the referee to allow players to continue to play after an infringement, if those with the ball can gain an advantage by doing so
All Blacks	Jonah Lomu played for the All Blacks, the New Zealand's national men's rugby team
attack	To move the ball forwards in order to score
backs	Numbers 9 - 15 of a team, the runners and tacklers in open play
beach rugby	an alternative to tag rugby, using similar rules, played with a size 4 ball on a beach, no shoes allowed and boys and girls can play together
box kick	A kick taken by the scrum half when facing his own team (generally near a ruck, maul or scrum), when he kicks the ball high over his shoulder in the direction of the opposition to surprise them
chip and chase	To give a short shallow kick over or around your opponent, then chase after it and hopefully gather it and continue to move forwards
clearance kick	A kick taken during play to move the ball quickly down the pitch, sometimes a *punt* sometimes a *drop kick*
conversion	A kick for goal after scoring a try, for two extra points on the scoreboard
converted try	A combination of a try and a conversion scoring seven points
core values	The RFU prides itself on its core values: Teamwork, Respect, Enjoyment, Discipline and Sportsmanship - essential to keeping the game safe and enjoyable for all
crossbar	The horizontal bar that connects the goalposts, conversion kicks and penalty field goals must go above this bar, not below it, to score points
dangerous play	Any action that could injure another player
dead ball line	The line behind the goalposts - not more than 22 metres from the try line

drop goal (also field goal)	This is a drop kick through the goalposts and over the crossbar during normal play, scoring three points
drop kick	A kick in which the ball is dropped to the ground before being struck with the foot
drop out	A kick taken from the 22-metre line after the ball has gone dead behind the dead ball line
field goal	see *drop goal*
forwards	Numbers 1-8 in the team who compete for the ball at scrums and line-outs and carry and move the ball through mauls, rucks and open play
forward pass	An illegal pass thrown to a position ahead of the player who threw it
foul	An infringement of the laws; illegal play
goal (1)	A successful kick between the goalposts and over the crossbar that earns two points for a conversion and three points for a penalty kick
goal (2)	The H-shaped structures at each end of the pitch with two upright *goalposts* and a *crossbar*
goal line (or try line)	The lines at each end of the pitch on which the goalposts are erected
goalposts	A rugby goal is shaped like the letter 'H', and the goalposts are the two vertical posts connected by a crossbar
grubber kick	A short shallow kick past an opponent along the ground which will force the opposition to stop and turn. The defence may find it more difficult to collect or gather the ball from the ground
half	A period of play lasting 40 minutes
halfway line	A line across the pitch 50 metres from each try line
hand off	A defensive technique involving the ball carrier pushing away the tackler with an open palmed hand, illegal with a straight arm, the attacking player can only use a bent arm in this move
high tackle	A dangerous tackle above the shoulder of the ball carrier

IRB	International Rugby Board - the lead organisation for rugby around the world
kick-off	A drop kick to start a period of play, i.e. at the start of each half, or after a team has scored a try
knock-on	A foul of knocking or dropping the ball forward onto the ground, towards the opposition
linesman/ lineswoman	The referee's assistants who run up and down the touch lines, one for each touch line
line-out	A formation of two lines of forwards with a channel between them into which the ball is thrown to restart play after the ball goes into touch
maul	A convergence of players around a ball carrier to push him and the ball forward with the ball OFF the ground
mini rugby	A game played by young children with less contact than the full game
obstruction	A foul of obstructing a player by blocking, tripping, shirt-pulling, etc.
offside	Touching the ball whilst on the opposition side of the previous ball player in your team; an illegal move which is penalised
pack	The forwards are frequently referred to as 'the pack'
pass	A legal throw of the ball to a team-mate
penalty kick	A free kick awarded by the referee that can be used to kick for goal, or over the touch line without possession
penalty try	A try awarded by the referee when he feels that a foul or series of fouls have been deliberately committed to prevent a try being scored
pitch	The playing field on which rugby is played. Most pitches are grassed, though some have surfaces of clay, sand or even snow

place kick	A kick taken by placing the ball on the pitch, stepping back and then moving in and kicking it. Before taking a place kick, some players use sand, a small hole dug into the pitch, a mound of earth, or a plastic tee to position the ball
punt	A kick in which the ball is dropped from the hand and kicked before it touches the ground. Often used in open play to gain ground. Also used when a penalty is awarded, to kick the ball into touch
put-in	The action of the scrum-half placing the ball into the scrum
red card	A card shown to a player being sent off the pitch for the rest of the game
RFU	Rugby Football Union - the English management organisation
ruck	A pack of linked players that forms over a ball to push the opposing team backward and gain control of the ball. Rucks usually start after a tackle, but they can start whenever the ball is loose ON the ground
Rugby League	The breakaway rugby code that was set up originally to allow players to earn money from the game
Rugby Sevens	The form of Rugby Union with only seven players per team, played over much shorter time-scales than the full team game
Rugby Union	The rugby code that used to be for amateur players only, though now professionals can also play - the most popular form of rugby in the world today
scrum/scrummage	A set play for forwards during which the ball is contested for on the ground by the hookers from both teams
sending off	The red-card penalty for which a player must leave the pitch for the rest of the game

sin bin	The area off the pitch where a player must wait for 10 minutes while serving a yellow card punishment
tackle	Action taken to stop a player from running with the ball. Ideally tackles take place around and below the waistline. Above the shoulders they are illegal *high tackles*
tap tackle	A tackle made by tapping the back of the runner's legs or feet to upset his balance and cause him to trip up
tag rugby	A version of the game for girls and boys, playing together or separately, and as a training system for older players. It involves wearing a tag belt that holds a 'tag' which counts as a tackle when it is removed from the wearer's belt
throw-in	The action of the hooker throwing the ball over and between the two rows of forwards at a line-out
touch	The area outside the two touch lines on either side of the pitch. A ball is said to be *in touch* when it is in this area
touch line	One of two lines that form the long sides of the playing area. The touch judges run along the touch lines and signal when the ball goes out. Supporters usually stand on the touch lines too
touch judge	The referees' assistant and the official who raises a flag if the ball goes into touch and indicates which side should be given the ball to throw-in at a line-out
touch rugby	A form of rugby in which players stop opponents from running with the ball by touching them lightly with a hand instead of tackling; used at junior level as a starting game and at senior level to increase handling skills
try	The act of taking the ball over the try line and grounding it with downward pressure to earn five points

try line	The line at each end of the pitch on which the goalposts are erected (see *goal line*) which should generally be passed in order for a try to be scored (however a ball on the line will also count as a try)
tunnel	The gap between and below the front rows in a scrum that the scrum-half puts the ball into at a scrum
veteran's rugby	A version of the game designed for older players, based on the standard 15-a-side game but with uncontested scrums and a recommendation that it should not be taken too seriously. Aggressive tackles are not welcomed.
wheeling the scrum	The act of deliberately moving the scrum round to put one team offside.
yellow card	The card shown by the referee to a player being cautioned for dangerous play which didn't result in an injury. A yellow card is also often shown for a deliberate or 'professional' foul, committed to prevent a try being scored. The players is sent off the pitch for ten minutes, to the *sin bin*
XV	Latin for fifteen - as in 1st XV team at school or club

Want to Learn More?

This reference list of websites will allow anyone interested in getting more involved in rugby the chance to explore it in more detail. We cannot take any responsibility for the accuracy of the links below which may alter after publication, but hopefully most are long-lived websites that will continue for many years to come.

Main website:

www.irb.org

The IRB supplies full information on how to play, the Laws that govern the game, full training techniques and pretty much anything you want to know about Rugby Union.

Other useful websites for information on rugby:

http://www.rugbyfootballhistory.com

http://www.englishclub.com/vocabulary/sports-rugby.htm

http://www.livestrong.com/kick-ball/

http://www.activenewzealand.com/resources/rugby-rules.php

http://www.teachpe.com/rugby/index.php

http://superskyrockets.hubpages.com/hub/Rugby-League-vs-Rugby-Union

http://en.wikipedia.org/wiki/Rugby_union

http://www.differencebetween.net/miscellaneous/differences-between-rugby-and-football/

http://www.schoolsrugby.co.uk/

http://www.rugbystuff.com/

http://www.bbc.co.uk/sport/0/rugby-union/

http://www.rbs6nations.com

http://www.rfu.com

http://www.wru.co.uk

http://www.scottishrugby.org

http://www.rugby.com.au/

http://www.allblacks.com/

http://www.nzru.co.nz/

http://www.nzrugby.co.nz/

http://www.sarugby.net/

http://www.usarugby.org

http://www.rugbycanada.ca/

http://www.uar.com.ar/

This list is not exhaustive and you can, of course, search the web for your local Rugby Union website, for national teams and other sides throughout Europe and worldwide, and for more information on your own team.

Kit suppliers

http://www.sportsdirect.com/rugby

http://www.surridgesport.co.uk/

http://www.genesissports.co.uk

http://www.kukrisports.com/gb-rugbyunion

http://www.rugbyspecialist.com/

http://www.kitbag.com/stores/kitbag/rugby.aspx

http://www.rugbyunionshirt.com

http://www.sportsworldrugby.co.uk

http://www.airosportswear.com/

http://www.viper10.com//rugby-kit-gallery

SUE PORTER'S NOTES

This year's team positions - complete in pencil to allow for re-use. We've allowed for up to 4 players for multiple friends and family:

Name		Position	
Name		Position	
Name		Position	
Name		Position	
Rugby Coach(es) this season:			
Points system for the current season:			
Try			
Conversion			
Drop Goal			
Penalty kick			

SUE PORTER'S GUIDE TO GAME SCORES

Fixture versus & date	Home or away	School/ Club Score	Opp. score	Our player's score	Comments
Example School 24.10.12	*A*	*12*	*13*	*6 (2 pens.)*	*Good game – only two tries though and both scored by the opposition*

Useful at the end of the season when reports need to be handed in. These will greatly endear your youngster or partner to his or her team Captain, who is frequently given the job of supplying such details to the sports master or team coach.

IF YOU'VE ENJOYED THIS BOOK, WHY NOT LOOK OUT FOR OUR NEXT OFFERINGS - COMING SOON:

SUE PORTER'S GUIDES TO . . .

CRICKET   Due out 2013

FOOTBALL   Due out 2013-2014

NETBALL and BASKETBALL

HOCKEY and LACROSSE

Check out our website www.sueportersguide.com for more links and information on all these games.

LAW UPDATE

From the 2012-13 season, referee instructions at scrums changed to:
Crouch, Touch, Set
This relates to the section on page 47 of this book. They have simply eliminated the "hold" stage from this set piece.

LAW UPDATE - 2013-14 SEASON

New engagement rules are being trialled globally. The new scheme requires referees to say: Crouch, Bind (the two packs come together), then Set. Once the packs are steady, the referee will say 'yes nine' at which time the scrum half will put the ball into the scrum straight and the packs can push against each other. It is hoped this will reduce scrum collapses.